the
friendship
band

by melanie ross mills

A purpose-based approach to connecting in friendship.

"The purpose-based friend changes the meaning of life. The purpose-based friend breathes life into the mundane, gives unspoken courage to deep-seated fears, and provides support to face life's challenges head on." —Melanie Ross Mills

The Friendship Bond
Second Edition
Copyright © 2013 by Melanie Ross Mills

Library of Congress Cataloging-in-Publication Data
Mills, Melanie Ross
The Friendship Bond / Melanie Ross Mills Productions
ISBN-13: 978-0-9882474-4-4
Self Help – Inspiration Relationship

ACKNOWLEDGMENTS

To my favorite purpose-based friend and husband, Michael. You are the love of my life. To my son, Michael Jr., my saving grace. You both teach me about love and friendship each and every day. You bless me beyond measure. You make me a better person. I love you always.

To Mom, Dad, Kath and Ed, Leila and Dick. To Anna, Jimmy, Elizabeth, Kim, Christine, Ellen, Cristin, Sara, Ashley, Laura, and Katie. To Lisa, Leslie, Julie, Sam, Shannon, and Punky. To Elisabeth, Robin, Bill, David, Rob, and Karen. To Alex, Lisa, Anne and Laurie, Stephanie and Laura.

To my family and friends over the years that have loved me no matter what I did or didn't do, said or didn't say; I appreciate and love you. You make the world a better place!

To all of you whom I have unintentionally hurt over the years and to those of you whom I will unintentionally hurt in the future, I am sorry. Thank you for extending grace and forgiveness to me. I will need it the rest of my life.

CONTENTS

INTRODUCTION

A Purpose-Based friendship is one founded on mutual trust, intentional investment, reciprocated exchange, and healthy boundaries. The purpose-based friendship provides each friend the freedom to love with vulnerability because they know that the other person is safe.

Every woman longs for these purpose-based friendships. We want friends with whom we can be vulnerable and those whom we can trust. Some of us have many purpose-based friendships; some of us have a few; some of us may not have any. *The Friendship Bond* intends to help move current friendships to be purpose-based. It also intends to guide the reader in the formation of new friendships where mutual trust and respect are the basis of the friendship.

This process begins with YOU. You have begun a journey of growing in purpose-based friendship. Congratulations for taking this step! More fulfillment and joy in your friendships are just around the corner.

The Friendship Bond will guide you through the following:

Friendship Foundation

- Learn about yourself, your personality, and what makes you uniquely you!

- Learn the difference between *knowing* about your strengths and *owning* the unique gifts you have to offer the world.

- Learn about yourself for a more complete under-standing of what you bring into your friendships.

Safe versus Unsafe Friendships

- Learn about using discernment when choosing your friends.

- Learn how to recognize which of your friends handle your heart with care and how to form authentic connections in the context of safe friendships.

- Learn how to give and how to receive. Learn the importance of reciprocating and the value in knowing how to place healthy boundaries in your friendships.

Expectations

- Learn how to wade through the waters of expectations. What does it mean to place unrealistic expectations on your friends?

Basic Needs

- Learn how we all have the same basic needs and how this affects every friendship in your life.

Intentional Choosing

- Learn how to be mindful when deciding which friends are healthy choices for you.

Friendship Choices

- Learn how to better understand and recognize which friendships are balanced and which are not.

My Journey

I will share my personal journey in friendship, from the time I was young through adulthood. Much of what I have learned about friendship will be woven into my personal story. (The exact details of my personal stories and the names of those in the stories have been modified in order to protect those involved.) Then, I will lead you in thinking about your personal friendship journey.

Your Journey

In each chapter we will examine the meaning and purpose of friendship, and then consider how you view friendship. At the end of each chapter, you will be given a list of questions, which are provided for introspection, to help you gain personal insight and enlightenment. We will answer these general questions:

- Are you maturing in the way you relate to your friends?

- Have you found that some friendships no longer work for you while others spring up in unexpected places?

- Do you have purpose-based friendships in your life?

Dates with Friends Option

The Friendship Bond, Dates with Friends companion book is the perfect opportunity to redefine your current view of friendship *with your friends*. How do you show love to each other? Can you each see the good in yourself and in your friendships? The companion book helps you grow together in learning about purpose-based friendship.

Bonding in friendship does not depend on your age, status, or present life circumstances. You may be fully content and loving life, running smoothly on all cylinders, or you may be going through incredibly difficult struggles that make it hard to hold your head above water.

No matter where you find yourself today—surrounded by friends or totally alone—the reality is that we all need *friendship bonds*, in the good times and in the bad. Life has its ups and downs, which is why we should intentionally learn about ourselves and connecting with friends.

If you would like to bring your friends with you on this journey of discovery, the *Date with Friends* companion book is the perfect opportunity to do so. In this book, you first learn about the different friend types you might have encountered along the way, from The Feels Like Home Friend to The Topper.

Then, you will select and invite your group of friends to go on a series of dates that correspond to the chapters in this book. These dates are designed to promote connection and bonding, and to assist you in forming purpose-based friendships. There will be discussion questions and talking points intended to instigate discussion between the group members. You are encouraged to tailor-make each date. Hopefully, after each date, you will learn new things about yourself and see yourself and others in a new light—a light that has broadened and enriched your life and your friendships.

Details on starting a group of your own can be found on page 159.

MESSAGE FROM MELANIE

I wrote *The Friendship Bond* because I want to share with you what I have learned about friendship over the years. It took me many years to realize that most of my friendships throughout my life had been *all about me*. I regret my unappreciative and self-entitled responses to thoughtful gestures and generous gifts. I am sad that I did not see these gestures as the selfless offering of time and energy that they were. I assume full responsibility for my immature and selfish ways. Somehow, I missed the memo on considering the feelings of my girlfriends on a consistent basis—the memo that should have taught me to love and care tenderly for their hearts. I needed to see and encourage them in their strengths and not take them for granted.

Unfortunately, I think that few of us are taught how to cultivate purpose-based friendships. Thankfully, over time, I have learned that good friendship is like a tenderly cared-for garden that, if weeded regularly, watered, and watched over, can grow an array of vibrant flowers that give its gardener great joy. I needed to spend time watering and caring for my

---

13

friendships (and yes, sometimes weeding) so that they would have the opportunity to bloom and offer me the connection for which I longed.

I had to learn how to *own* my strengths. To me, identity was just an overused spy-movie term. Bond, James Bond, had his own unique identity as 007, and I was very happy for him, but I could not have told you my own! I didn't realize I must first understand and care for myself before I could appreciate, offer grace, and care for my friends. You know the old cliché: "You cannot love others until you learn to love yourself?" Well, I needed to learn how to do both—love myself and love others.

As I uncovered my unique strengths and personality traits, I began to understand what I had to offer my friends. I learned more about myself and became more secure in how I was uniquely created. As I did this, I was set free to accept, love, and embrace those around me.

Today, I have experienced some of the most meaningful, authentic, and purpose-based friendships. I have opened my heart up to safe friends that care tenderly for me. They encourage me in my strengths and give me grace for my weaknesses. They point out when I have cast the line too far, and they help reel me back in gently. As I have grown in purpose-based friendship, I have chosen friends who I respect and admire. I want to be more like them in many ways. Why have I chosen these types of women? Because I believe the old adage:

"One will become like who they are with."

> ### Reproducing
>
> If you want to know what you will look like in five years, just look at who you are hanging out with today.
>
> This is the relationship version of – "*You are what you eat.*"

My hope is that once you have completed this book, and hopefully the *Dates with Friends* companion book, you will find a newfound security in naturally making wiser friend choices. You will no longer need to be prettier, most intelligent, or have all of the answers. You will begin seeking out those that are more intelligent and kind and gentle and peaceful and loving and patient. You will be drawn to those friends that are stable and dependable, to those who are more enlightened and secure. You will respect them because of their integrity, high character, and grace. And you will want to know these people better. You will then choose friends because you want all of these traits for yourself.

Secure in your own identity and place in the process of growing in purpose-based friendship, you will be drawn to others with this same perspective, and they will be drawn to you. Possibly, for once in your life, you will be drawn to lifeboats instead of sinking ships.

"Maybe that's why they call them friend-SHIPS?"

CHAPTER 1

THE FIRST FRIEND

My Journey

I was just five years old the first time I thought I saw an angel. Standing on my front porch, I saw a small figure coming down the street—a perfect little girl—a blue-eyed blonde with long curling lashes on a china doll face. As she neared, I stood frozen. She gracefully ascended the steps to my house as though she needed no steps at all.

Breathless, transfixed by her beauty, I said nervously, "Melanie, my name is Melanie. We just moved in."

"Hi, Melanie. I'm Anna," she replied.

In this five-year-old girl Anna, I found my first friend and discovered what a delightful thing friendship could be.
From that day forward, Anna and I were inseparable. We were like peanut butter and jelly, Oprah and Gayle, Hershey's

and Kisses. We were thick as thieves. We exchanged friend-ship bracelets, beads, and charms. We had a theme for every day of the week; because not a moment went by that we did not want to be together. We had movie night Monday, dress up Tuesday, waterpark Wednesday, talent show Thursday (I always had first pick in the costume drawer), freedom Friday, and Six Flags Saturday. We took dancing together, did cheerleading, and even attempted French and Spanish at some point.

As we grew, so did the sophistication of our play. One year, we said we were older than we were so that we could go with the cool, older kids to their camp one summer. It was a church camp, and we lied in order to be able to go. Don't worry -we did get caught- and, no, I am not proud of it! What made us think that breaking a major Biblical commandment—*do not lie*—would bode well for us in trying to go to a camp where everyone knew us from home?

From the inside jokes to the matching outfits, sleepovers, and times we insisted we were sick of one another, Anna was my first best friend. And in the innocence of my child's heart, I genuinely believed she would be my last. Little did I know that things were about to change . . . in a big way.

Our friendship romance lasted five years. No competition and no new neighbors to break up the bliss of our routine. Then we entered middle school, and everything began to change.

Although we had outer circle friends before, no one had been able to break the best-friend bond. Nor had we wanted them to. Imagine my surprise when a new girl came to town. Her name was Carina.

We were in sixth grade, and she was quite lovely. Carina had the allure of being "not from home," and we all flocked to her for some knowledge of "the other world." She not only brought stories of another life but was also everything a girl wants to be: bubbly, precocious, kind, gentle, caring, smart, and simply beautiful.

Through the grapevine and with the absence of my best friend confirming the rumors, I finally understood that someone else had taken my place in Anna's life. Just as she had effortlessly floated into my life eight years before, so she floated out that year, and into the life of another, Carina.

There was nothing not to like about Carina—Anna had chosen well (of course, she had chosen me too!)—but it was heart wrenching to know that waterpark Wednesdays and talent show Thursdays were no longer mine to share with her. My heart had broken.

Since I had never had another best friend and did not know that you could have more than one, I felt only confusion. I had been betrayed and abandoned. This was my very first breakup, the first time that I had experienced the feeling of rejection. I cried many tears and spent hours gazing out of my bedroom window, hoping to watch that angel glide back down my path and into my playroom.

Try as I might to understand, deep down I knew to wait this one out. And so I waited, every day wondering when Anna would come to her senses and miss me. "Surely she will want me back!" I thought. To relieve my anguish while I waited, I decided to stay very busy with the B team. We went to the movies and the mall; we had sleepovers. As distracting as the other girls could be, my heart only ached. And even as each day passed and I did not hear from Anna, I could not shake the belief that she would, any day, ring my doorbell and present me with our season passes to the water park.

If I could have only seen that sunshine always comes after the rain. My field of vision was limited due to my limited experience in friendship. And then, just like the sunshine, one day, it happened! But it wasn't quite as I had planned. (By the way, it never is.) Anna returned to my doorstep. But she didn't bring the season passes I expected. At first, I felt disappointed, until I realized what she did bring—something far better—Anna returned with a whole new group of best friends!

She had not forgotten about me! She had come back! And the new girls, well, they were equally as beautiful and loving as Carina. And they were now mine to share in friendship.

With each passing year, the group expanded—from Cassidy to Christie to Stacey to Britt to Abby to Kim to Susan to Caroline. Having a big group of friends just added to the fun and excitement of being together.

Anna had not left me after all. From the day of her return, I began to understand that I might not always be her first pick for waterpark Wednesday or movie night Monday. And I was okay with that. I had begun to experience the joy of having several friends with the same interests and unique personalities. This was my first friendship lesson in sharing, letting go, and being open to change.

Friendship Foundation

As they say, there is a first time for everything. Anna was my first friend, first choice, first heartbreak, first taste of not being first, and first teacher in learning friendship lessons and in observing opportunities for growth in friendship. This was the beginning of my friendship foundation.

All friendships have a starting point—some friendships may come through mutual friends, others may go all the way back to math class in elementary school. Once two people realize they want to be friends, they normally begin to get to know each other, and later they make a choice to pursue this friendship more long term. This choice does not always seem like a conscious decision, but it is nonetheless a decision each person has made, whether or not they can point to that "deciding" time.

The underpinnings of friendship form the foundation that each friendship is based upon. A person can develop a solid

Underpinning
The material and construction (foundation) used for support of a structure.

or a faulty foundation in friendship. I did not know the difference for many, many years.

The underpinning of a solid foundation consists of two people having a mutual understanding and sharing equally in respect and love for each other. As these aspects of friendship are cultivated and tended to, the trust between the two friends grows and expands, producing an attachment or bond that is irreplaceable. This type of friendship foundation is built on rock, not sand, and a loyal, trustworthy friendship is formed.

Faulty Foundation

The opposite can also occur in friendship. A friendship can be built upon a foundation of dishonesty, mistrust, and selfish gain (all wrapped up in what might look like love for a little while, but is really just self-serving). The attachments and bonds that are formed are temporary and breakable.

This foundation is built on sand, not on rock. Anything that one person does not like or approve of can change the loyalty, commitment, and devotion of one or both friends involved.

Throughout this book, you will learn what is necessary to form a solid friendship foundation, which will result in purpose-based friendship.

Before we can build our foundation, we must be clear as to the definition of friendship. According to Merriam-Webster's Dictionary, a friend is:

One who is attached to another by affection or esteem:
An acquaintance;
One that is not hostile;
A favored companion.

When I first encountered this definition of friendship, I knew I had not known how to be this type of friend on a consistent basis. This led me to think that maybe there should be a required class on friendship—one semester of learning how to be a purpose-based friend (classroom), one semester of applying purpose-based friendship qualities out in the world (lab work), and one semester of an internship in friendship. If I had done this, maybe I would have seen all of the friendship baggage I carried around, not the least of which was a continual fear of being rejected by my friends.

Unwittingly, I had given Anna the power to dictate how I would perceive other friends that came into my life. She had taught me to fear rejection, and I did not know I was worthy of being someone else's friend. Even when I realized that someone had, indeed, chosen me to be her friend, I never fully understood the reasons why.

I gradually realized I needed to understand what I had to offer others and what they could offer me. Armed with this knowledge, I would be able to make the most of the friendship learning opportunities that came my way. Anna also taught me some beautiful lessons in friendship—ones that I have held with me since I was a young girl. From her, I learned that . . .

- Angels need to fly—it's how they're made.
- I shouldn't put all my eggs in one basket.
- I can expect way too much out of one friendship.

- I can have more than one best friend.

- I can have different types of friends for different reasons and seasons.

- I cannot make a friend stay, not even a best friend, over many years.

- I might not be the first pick, and I might never get picked, but that's okay.

- *Friendship is a privilege and a choice.*

Anna showed me that if a friend chooses to float off into the sunset, God will always send a new friend along . . .

Once again,

"Maybe that's why they call them friend-SHIPS?"

Your Journey

Your very first friendship experience made some degree of impact on your life because it was your first. Reflect on your very first friendship—it is the first door to open to discover how to create great friendship foundations.

Who was your first best friend? _____

How old were you? _____

Where did you grow up? _____

Why did you choose this person to be your best friend? Explain.

_____

_____

_____

How did your best friend make you feel? Explain.

_____

_____

_____

Did you continue to grow closer or did you grow apart? Explain.

_____

_____

_____

What brought you closer or made you grow apart? Explain.

_____

_____

_____

Were you a loving first best friend? Explain.

_____

_____

_____

Looking back, is there anything you would have done differently? Explain.

_____

_____

_____

Have you learned your own first friend lesson along the way? Explain.

_____

_____

_____

_____

CHAPTER 2

RESPONSE CHECK

My Journey

Although my first friendship lesson with my little angel Anna was hurtful, I still continued growing and learning from my friendships. Alas, I learn things the hard way. The following story illustrates. . .

I met Kate in my mid-20s while we were both new to the corporate Dallas workplace. This was an era of personalized heavy card stock business cards, pencil skirts, pointed toe high heels and a beautiful strand of pearls (Each borrowed from our moms.). Together, we were going to take over corporate America. Kate was from Abilene, a small cattle town. I was from Dallas, a big city. We not only worked in the same office building in downtown Dallas, but we also rented apartments within walking distance from one another. And yes, these were the "single scene" apartments where all the "cool kids" would reside after college graduation.

Kate loved smoky bars and techno dance clubs; I loved small group dinners and spontaneous karaoke nights. Considering our differences, Kate was one of the most interesting people I had met in a while.

I guess that college was her entry into becoming cultured and "in the know." Kate knew a little about everything. She loved to paint and write; she subscribed to *The New York Times*, and had friends living all over — just like a regular New Yorker. We attended events, movies, shared friends and shopped together. I was Kate's nurse on sick days and she spent holidays with my family. After two years, we were the best of friends.

Unfortunately, one night while she was out dancing, Kate met a boy. This was a "fabulous" boy and overnight I was replaced. The romance blossomed, Kate stopped calling, and our friendship discontinued. I had given her two years of my life! I had trusted her with my fears and joys. She would be my maid of honor. She was in my all-time, top-ten list. I was perplexed. And again, I found myself heartbroken.

I would like to think everyone would love to be my friend —

but I know this is not the case. A friend I loved and trusted with my heart dropped me in the grease, cold turkey!

This deeply hurt me. I wept, felt depressed and so hurt. I loved Kate deeply and felt so deeply rejected that I questioned my own value as a friend. Sometimes, as you will read in future chapters, we choose unsafe friends. If any friend did not handle your heart properly, you will have the opportunity to lay down these past hurts and ban them from future friendships.

Broken Trust

One way I began healing was realizing I was not the only person that had been "de-friended" by a best friend. I recalled a situation I had experienced when I was around 19 years old, during the second semester of my junior year at the University of Texas at Austin. (Yes, I am a proud Texas Longhorn!) A sorority sister, Stephanie and I had become close friends. Stephanie had another friend as well named Anne who she met in her math class. They both loved exercising and partying together, going to the movies on the weekends and laughed together a lot. Often I encountered them at the same parties and they seemed very close. I did fear however how long the friendship would last. Anne was known for being fickle and bouncing from one friendship to the next.

Sure enough, Stephanie developed a huge crush on a new boy at school, Christopher. However, Christopher liked Anne. Anne knew that Stephanie really liked Christopher. (I didn't want to get involved and kept my mouth shut.) Before long, Christopher and Anne were dating. I really felt for Stephanie as she called me crying and confused. Her heart-break was double —Christopher did not like *her* and Anne had ditched their friendship for a boy!

From that day on Stephanie became increasingly skeptical and distrustful of women and their intentions. Future friends complained she was "guarded." Stephanie had not healed from her past hurt and blamed herself. She trusted no one and distanced herself even from trustworthy friends, including me — our friendship ended. I encouraged Stephanie to try understanding what Anne was really like as a friend and what their friendship was truly based on. Through introspection, Stephanie could have learned how to assess her ability to discern how to choose wisely. Unfortunately, an opportunity for growth was not utilized.

My Response

Just like Stephanie, I also experienced a wake-up call to get my friendship booty in gear after Kate. I noticed I was carrying past hurts into my friendships. I was overreacting when I felt hurt or rejected. I called this "My Response Check."

As I considered my responses to hurtful or difficult situations with people, I tried analyzing my emotional response and believed it was always about me and something I had done wrong, or some quality in me that provoked the bad treatment or situation in the first place. I analyzed my own emotional responses to determine what was my true trigger for feeling the way I did? If I felt bitter or unforgiving for instance, I could see that I was harboring anger. If I was quick to anger, I was probably experiencing hurt. If I was tempted to share a story that would place my friend in a "not so great" light, I was probably jealous or threatened. I did a "response check" to pay attention to my responses on a daily basis. I still do and I highly recommend it.

Just like Stephanie's response to Anne, my response to Kate leaving me cold turkey was unhealthy. I wallowed in self-pity and allowed her choices to dictate how I saw myself. This made me feel unworthy of any friendship. I would question whether I was a good friend to her and what did I lack that other friends offered?

Knowing Myself

I needed to rebound and heal from past friendship hurts. I also needed to no longer assess my value on the basis of her approval of me. (This empowered her too much and de-valued me.) I considered myself a failure because of her rejection — which I knew in my heart was ludicrous. One way I turned the situation around was using the situation as an opportunity to work on my weaknesses. I analyzed why I'd befriended Kate to be sure I wouldn't make a similar bad decision. I realized I was a codependent friend. Talk about putting all my eggs in the wrong basket!

This disguised blessing of hurt and pain taught me that what I brought to a friendship was just as important *if not more important* than what the friendship brought to me. I couldn't control my friends and their behavior. I could control whom I befriended.

I also evaluated whether I was evaluating this friendship on the basis of who they are, or, am I viewing them through the lens of my past hurts? I then evaluated what I have to offer Kate, even if she couldn't see it for herself.

Your Journey

Has a friend you thought hung the moon rejected you and broken your heart? If so, you also know this is one of the best things to have ever happened to you. This may also referred to your response to breakup with a boyfriend who dumps you for no reason — preferring just to "be friends." While you are crying in your coffee, you don't even realize that Prince Charming is right around the corner.

Now take some time to do your own "Response Check."

Have you considered your outward responses to situations may indicate deeper feelings in your heart?

If so, name a situation in which you realized your initial reaction revealed something deeper was going on.

_____

_____

_____

_____

_____

_____

If no instance comes to mind, you can still pay attention to your responses and what they say about your true feelings. This will be the key to healing from past friendship hurts and entering new friendships healthy and whole!

Additional Thoughts:

_____

_____

_____

_____

_____

_____

_____

_____

_____

_____

_____

_____

_____

_____

_____

_____

_____

_____

_____

CHAPTER 3

OWNING YOUR STRENGTHS

My Journey

After my debacle with Kate I was determined not to respond so negatively again. I achieved this by seeking not only to *learn about* but also to *own* my strengths therefore better understanding my worth and value.

We each process our own sparkling identity making us unique and demonstrating our importance. We each have our own specific purpose, which is why we provide value and worth to the world at large.

> ### Worth
> The value of something measured by its qualities or by the esteem in which it is held.

Yet I question whether we truly believe beauty is within our hearts. Many of us simply don't believe, or we want to believe but don't know how.

I grew up with a mom that constantly told me that my life mattered. She made me feel as if I could accomplish any goal or task if I were willing to put in the effort. I also had teachers that made me feel valued and wanted. Although I had self-confidence, it was performance based.

Sometimes, I was misguided about where my worth came from. I believed my worth was based on my performance and external attributes (and of course, my charming personality!). For others it could be their grades, accomplishments, occupation, degrees, pedigree, intellect, physical appearance, or their ability to influence. Or perhaps others take to heart the message that their worth derives from being perfect and right. If we internalized these messages, then as adults we need to be validated by this same framework or grid of measure. The messages we receive about ourselves can play an important role in which adults we become.

As I started to understand that my worth was not based on what I did, said, looked like, or accomplished, I was free to embrace the truth that my worth was based solely on the fact that I was a human being, created by God! And this was not just for me, but for every human being walking on this earth!

Each of us has a reason for breathing! We all have a purpose as to why we are here on this earth. We have a contribution to make just by becoming who we were *truly* meant to be.

This is *not* about the power of the mind or positive thinking to make yourself into the person you want to become. This is *not* about becoming prideful in your strengths so that you can walk around feeling as if you are "better than" those around you. This is *not* about inflating your ego. This *is* about knowing your intrinsic worth, associated gifts, and personal strengths.

And… this is where freedom in knowing your individual identity begins!

My Worth

In order to be truly happy and have fulfilling friendships I had to start believing the truth about myself—that I was worthy. This flowering process was beautiful – the more I understood my uniqueness, the more I embraced my weaknesses. I did this without fearing I was less or bad. On the contrary, identifying my weaknesses made my future friendships healthy and long-lasting.

A close friend of mine says, "Sometimes we can be a lousy source of truth for ourselves." I agree and believe the first step in building better friendship foundations is gaining a clearer understanding of ourselves so we can play to our strengths and gifts instead of trying to become someone we are not.

I know this isn't easy, especially when you've been hurt. It is also more challenging to reengineer and un-train many years of wrong thinking. But it is vital to love yourself so that you can grow in your friendships.

Your Journey

Your perception of who you are will influence how you think, feel, and respond to people and circumstances.

If you think you have little value when someone pokes fun at you, you're more likely to internalize what they say and take it personally. If, on the other hand, you know you are unique and uniquely gifted, if someone is sarcastic about you, you can shrug it off, laugh and remember who you really are!

It may be easier to focus on and own your individual strengths. By *owning your strengths* and *knowing your intrinsic worth*, you have more to offer your friendships and those around you. If you struggle seeing your strengths, it is important others around you remind you of your worth.

If you received mixed messages growing up—for example, if you were raised by perfectionist parents or an abusive family offering you little encouragement and causing you verbal, physical or emotional pain—you may play those old tapes in your head. You may feel nothing you do is ever good enough. This is a lie, and more the subject of being torn down in the past than anything based in reality.

There are two parts to this reflection time: the first asks you to assess yourself, and the second asks you to consult your loved ones for their view on what are your strengths. Have fun, and take time to hear the truth about how others see you, in case you can't always see it for yourself!

Part 1

In what areas of your life do you excel (hint: think of things you love to do)?

_____

_____

In what circumstances do others tend to come to you for help? *

_____

_____

*Recall examples when serving or helping others comes easily to you. *When helping comes easily, you are operating in your strengths.*

_____

Write down three of your strengths. (Hint: Think about what you like about yourself!)

Strength

_____

Strength

_____

Strength

_____

Part 2

Ask three friends or family members to share with you one or two strengths they see in you. (Hint: Give them a deadline so they will respond promptly.)

Here is a sample note:

Dear _____ ,

I am reading The Friendship Bond. *The assignment is to ask three of my friends or family members to share with me a few strengths that*

they have witnessed in my life. Would you please share a few strengths
that you have seen in me?

Thank you so much!

Strengths seen by others:

_____

_____

_____

_____

_____

_____

_____

_____

_____

_____

_____

_____

_____

_____

_____

_____

CHAPTER 4

TEMPERAMENT

My Journey

I became curious about what place friendship had in my life and what were my individual strengths. I wondered for instance, why did one friend love to serve at the food pantry while the other chose to counsel someone by phone?

- Why did one friend like to lead the service project while the other preferred serving behind the scenes?

- As for me, why did I feel anxious when I volunteered in the nursery, but loved people feeling that they could trust me?

- Where did these unique, individualized strengths that I witnessed in myself and others come from?

I was soon to be rewarded for my Sherlock Holmes stealth. One Sunday morning, while living in Houston, my friend called me in a panic. She was in a jam and needed me to volunteer on her behalf the following weekend. Of course, I wanted to help! Yet as she told me what precisely the work entailed, my palms started to sweat. She needed me in the nursery—the one place I do not like volunteering. I love babies, and adore children but babies freak me out. I worry whether I can settle them. And what if it was feeding time? Oh no! Would the milk be warm enough? Would I hold the baby correctly? And even worse- what happens after the feeding takes place?!? Diaper changes are so gross! I worked myself into a panic before I hung up the phone. However, I knew it was the right thing to do. I agreed to help out and intended to follow through.

Somehow I made it. But my two hours in the nursery left me more confused. I wondered why my friend loved feeding babies and changing diapers while I was repelled. How could she sit and rock a crying baby while I found the sound nerve wracking? Why did she prefer tenderly loving babies while I thrived on taking my teenage niece for an up-do before a dance?"And this is what triggered my need to better understand precisely what makes us who we are.

In the thick of this exploration, I was at lunch with my girlfriends when one expounded on her distress that her hairdresser moved to another salon; another girl chatted about her tennis team choosing the wrong outfits; someone else mentioned wanting to adopt a child from Africa; another expounded on her terrific vacation to New York.

It was a lot to process, but this revealed how differently we each converse and our different interests. One person's interests or experience morphed our conversation in an entirely different direction. How did we segue from child adoption from Africa to hideous tennis outfits?

It was this colorful conversation that showed me how different and unique each of us is in our gifts. What one person loved, the other found miserable. What fulfilled one tormented another. Although we were close friends, we were all so different. As I took out my magnifying glass, I discovered each person has an individual temperament!

Temperament

The Oxford Dictionary defines one's *temperament* as

A person's nature, especially as it permanently affects their behavior.

In psychology, *temperament* refers to those aspects of an individual's personality, such as introversion or extroversion, which are often regarded as *innate rather than learned.*

A temperament reveals our God-given strengths (and weaknesses) that help make up our personality. Most of us are a blend of more than one temperament, but we usually have one dominant type.

Weakness

A weakness is an unmet need.

For Example:

An unmet need: A person with strong leadership qualities could misuse this strength by trying to control others in order to feel important and valued.

A met need: Once this person's need for significance is met by them knowing their identity and inherent self worth- their strength in leadership can operate without the misuse of trying to control others for validation.

Temperament helps explain peoples' actions and responses. As I learned about my own temperament, I was able to see and embrace my strengths, as well as understand my weaknesses.

This insight started helping me in my friendships because I became more aware, more understanding, and more appreciative of friends who differed from me. I saw more clearly their differences complemented my weaknesses and added to my strengths.

Your Journey

What Is Your Temperament?

The following activity offers insight into your own temperament and can provide a piece to your identity puzzle.

In the list below, check the boxes that apply to you. Add up the number of checked boxes at the end of each section.

Section 1

As a person, you

☐ Are a born leader   ☐ Are dynamic and active

☐ Are unemotional   ☐ Must correct wrongs

☐ Are strong-willed and decisive   ☐ Establish goals

☐ Have a strong need for change   ☐ Motivate others to action

☐ Can run anything   ☐ Exude confidence

☐ Are not easily discouraged   ☐ Exert sound leadership

☐ Are goal-oriented   ☐ Know the right answer

☐ Meet goals expected of you   ☐ Delegate work to others

□ See the whole picture □ Are organized

□ Thrive on opposition □ Seek practical solutions

□ Move quickly to action □ Excel in emergencies

□ Insist on production □ Have little need for friends

□ Are stimulated by activity

Total Number Checked Section 1: _____

Section 2

As a person, you

□ Have an appealing personality □ Are curious

□ Are talkative, a storyteller □ Are the life of the party

□ Have a good sense of humor □ Live in the present

□ Have a good memory for color □ Are good on stage

□ Thrive on compliments □ Love people

□ Are enthusiastic □ Have a sincere heart

□ Are cheerful □ Seem exciting to others

□ Are wide-eyed and innocent □ Make situations fun

□ Are expressive □ Apologize quickly

☐ Make friends easily	☐ Think up new activities
☐ Are liked by your friends	☐ Turn disaster into humor
☐ Like to volunteer for jobs	☐ Have a changeable disposition
☐ Value looking good	☐ Are creative and colorful
☐ Inspire others to join	☐ Have energy and enthusiasm
☐ Don't hold grudges	☐ Are flashy and showy at times
☐ Are tactile while speaking	

Total Number Checked Section 2: _____

Section 3

As a person, you

☐ Are deep and thoughtful	☐ Are analytical
☐ Are serious and purposeful	☐ Are highly intelligent
☐ Are talented and creative	☐ Are artistic or musical
☐ Are philosophical and poetic	☐ Appreciate beauty
☐ Are sensitive to others	☐ Are self-sacrificing
☐ Are conscientious	☐ Are idealistic
☐ Set high standards	☐ Do things the right way

☐ Keep your home in order   ☐ Pick up after others

☐ Sacrifice your own will for others   ☐ Are schedule-oriented

☐ Are detail conscious   ☐ Are neat and tidy

☐ Are a perfectionist   ☐ Have high standards

☐ Are persistent and thorough   ☐ Are orderly and organized

☐ Are economical   ☐ Identify problems easily

☐ Find creative solutions   ☐ Finish what you start

☐ Avoid attracting attention   ☐ Like charts, graphs, lists

☐ Make friends cautiously   ☐ Are faithful and devoted

Total Number Checked Section 3: _____

Section 4

As a person, you

☐ Are low-key   ☐ Are easygoing

☐ Are calm and collected   ☐ Are well-balanced

☐ Like consistency   ☐ Make time for your friends

☐ Are quiet but witty   ☐ Are sympathetic and kind

☐ Are happily reconciled to life   ☐ Keep emotions hidden

☐ Are an all-purpose person   ☐ Make a good friend

☐ Are not in a hurry   ☐ Take the good with bad

☐ Don't get upset easily   ☐ Are competent and steady

☐ Are peaceful and agreeable   ☐ Have administrative ability

☐ Are the peacemaker   ☐ Avoid conflicts

☐ Are good under pressure   ☐ Find the easy way

☐ Are easy to get along with   ☐ Are pleasant

☐ Are inoffensive   ☐ Are a good listener

☐ Have a dry sense of humor   ☐ Enjoy people watching

☐ Have many friends   ☐ Have compassion

Total Number Checked Section 4: _____

Double-check you have checked all the boxes of the personality traits you feel you possess.

Count up the items you checked in each section. Write that number at the bottom of each section, 1 through 4. Then, fill in the section numbers (1 through 4) below with the highest to the lowest number of boxes checked.

Highest Number: Section _____

Second Highest Number: Section _____

Third Highest Number: Section _____

Lowest Number: Section _____

Florence Littauer, author of *Your Personality Tree*, sees four personality temperaments: Choleric, Sanguine, Melancholy, and Phlegmatic. These are based on the findings of the old sage Hippocrates.

Now, let's learn your temperament! The section with the most checked boxes is your dominant type, and the section with the second most circled boxes will contribute to your "blend." Now let's see where your temperament falls:

- If you checked the most under Section 1, then your temperament is *Choleric*.
- If you checked the most under Section 2, then your temperament is *Sanguine*.
- If you checked under Section 3, then your temperament is *Melancholy*.
- If you checked the most under Section 4, then your temperament is *Phlegmatic*.

See if one of the subsequent temperament descriptions describes you!

The Choleric is	The Sanguine is
• An extrovert	• An extrovert
• A born leader	• Talkative
• Self-confident	• Positive
• A risk taker	• Friendly
• Appreciative of competence	• A people person
	• An attention seeker

The Melancholy is	The Phlegmatic is
• An introvert	• An introvert
• A deep thinker	• Observant
• Sensitive	• Charming
• Very caring	• Laid back
• Highly creative	• A good listener

It takes all kinds. There are beautiful, necessary strengths in each temperament.

As you think about your friends, these temperament

descriptions might help clarify why the <u>Choleric</u> friend can't help but lead the charge and tell everyone what to do for the holiday party. Or why the <u>Melancholy</u> friend might expect someone to include her in the lunch bunch. Or why the <u>Sanguine</u> friend acts like you have been best friends since kindergarten when you just met her yesterday. Or why the <u>Phlegmatic</u> friend will never co-lead a canned food drive. Now, maybe you won't take your friends' different decisions so personally . . . and you might even invite the melancholy friend to lunch!

Let's reflect on what you've just learned about yourself and how this relates to your friends.

You:

Did selecting certain traits remind you of strengths you'd forgotten?

_____

Where do you see your temperament traits being used in your life? Give at least one example.

_____

_____

Do you struggle with your temperament? For instance, if you're a Choleric, do you see yourself as a "born leader"? Or if you're a Phlegmatic, do you struggle seeing yourself as "charming"?

_____

_____

_____

What one quality of your temperament do you love most about yourself? Why?

_____

_____

_____

Your Friends:

What strengths do certain friends of yours have that complement your strengths?

_____

_____

_____

Do you encourage your friends to use their strengths? If so, how?

_____

_____

_____

Do you use the strengths of your friends to help others out? For example, try connecting a friend that is an encourager with a friend that wrestles with low self- esteem.

_____

_____

_____

How does understanding your strengths and your personality traits enable you to reach your full potential? Explain.

_____

_____

_____

_____

_____

_____

_____

_____

Understanding your strengths and personality traits will result in your being a better friend!

CHAPTER 5

SAFE OR UNSAFE?

My Journey

As I learned about my personality type and strengths, I also had the honor of learning about my weaknesses. I use the word *honor* intentionally. We often feel ashamed about our weaknesses. But I don't. I see my weaknesses as *opportunities for growth*. However, this does not come naturally to me; it is a discipline.

My weaknesses included saying insensitive things at inappropriate times. I sometimes in-advertently hurt people's feelings, or disappointed someone unknowingly. Five clear weaknesses I noticed in myself were:

- A need for discernment.

- A classic case of codependence.

- A fear of rejection.

- A need to forgive freely.

- A need for authentic communication (in Chapter 6).

I prioritized these weaknesses in terms of which ones I wanted to change and improve on the most.

Discernment

Looking back I saw the need for discernment early on, in my very first friendship with Anna. For instance, when Anna rejected my invitation to the mall, to the movies or to go shopping, I would continually invite her until she said yes. All the while, Anna was with Carina! I ignored she did not reciprocate my invitations; in fact, she did not only not reciprocate—she was never available when I initiated.

Once I learned the truth I felt dumb and took it personally she had been moonlighting, and everyone but me noticed. Many years after Anna had come and gone, I was back to square one then I met Patricia through mutual friends. I loved Patricia because she was insightful, wise, energetic, and patient. She had been recently derailed by circumstances outside of her control, and I wanted to help her get her life back on track.

I gave everything to help: I spent time with Patricia versus my family. I rearranged social engagements to include her and I opened up my personal life. We were inseparable.

Then, I heard rumors she was talking about me to others. I was incredulous at first. How could she love me and also gossip about me? That's crazy. Isn't it? I began questioning who she really was.

When a trusted friend showed me a text she had sent, and I saw Patricia's dishonesty first hand. I was heartbroken and confused. It took me several weeks, but I began seeing her poor decisions were about her and not a reflection of my friendship to her. It didn't matter how good a friend I was; I could not make her secure in herself or honest. I realized she had treated others this same way but I still felt I had been blindsided.

I questioned my own self worth, and wondered why on earth I chose (yet again) such a hurtful friend? How did I not learn my lesson? My other friends witnessed my pain, and one wise friend recommended a book called *Safe People*, by Henry Cloud. Merriam-Webster defines safe as

"not causing harm or injury"

Not causing harm or injury. I combined the words together—"safe" and "friend"—and realized that *a safe friend* would be one *who does not (intentionally) cause harm or injury.* I then wondered if *I* were a safe person. How was I supposed to know who is safe and who is not? As I transitioned to learning about my own internal strengths and value system, my knowledge about friendship fit like a piece in the puzzle.

I found Cloud's book riveting. In the very first chapter, Cloud writes, "We do not get a lot of training in evaluating character. We tend to look on the outside and not on the inside of a person."[1]

And there lay my *Aha* moment. I remembered God saying this very thing long before Mr. Cloud's wisdom . . . you know that verse in the Bible: *Man (or woman) looks on the outside but God looks at the heart?* I realized I had been looking on the outside when evaluating my friendships! I had not been evaluating these friends on the basis of character—their insides—but on their exterior and what they might offer me.

Growing up in America culture where looks, fame, affluence all count, I'd never looked beyond superficial qualities in new friends. Therefore, I had been repeatedly hurt.

Cloud continues by categorizing unsafe people as "the Abandoners, the Critics, and the Irresponsibles."[2] Once again, the heavens opened up and I saw the light! I had befriended abandoners, critics, and irresponsibles (and had, at times, been that myself)—no wonder I was wounded. I knew I couldn't change the characteristics of previous or current friends. But I could initiate change within myself.

As I identified my strengths, I recognized I had not operated from my strengths as a friend. I wanted to be all things to all people, not seeing that cleaning babies' bottoms was no strength of mine!

I also realized where in the past I had been the abandoner for one friend, the critic for another, and the irresponsible friend to many. This was a tough but necessary exercise. To be a different friend, I had to evaluate my performance as a friend.

When I finished Cloud's glorious book, I wept with relief. I had the tools to continue my growth and heal from past friendship hurts!

My Safe Friends

None of this is to dismiss how much God helped me before this *Aha* moment. God was smart enough to offer me a few safe friends along the way. The issue was I hadn't recognized these safe qualities, *because I had not yet valued or possessed them myself.* I also needed to become wiser about my personal value system and what truly mattered to me.

From this point I saw myself and others in a different light and began seeing what constituted safe versus unsafe. I reflected on what made someone trustworthy, how to avoid unhealthy relationships and form healthy ones.

Codependency

I vowed to desire not to hurt or injure a valued friend again. I began understanding my past codependent choices which led to hurt, worry and pain when I wrongfully felt responsible not just for my decisions, but for others too.

A month later, when a friend shared a reckless idea to start dating her best friend's boyfriend, I tried redirecting her focus elsewhere. Using the old adage, there are plenty of other fish in the sea. Her response blew me away: she believed I opposed her making this very poor decision *because I felt responsible for her choices.* She also believed that I thought it would reflect poorly on *me* if she proceeded with her hair-brained scheme. You know what? She was right! What an eye opener! I did feel responsible for her choices and I thought others might think I was in cahoots with her because we were so close. You want to know the twisted part? *I needed her to need me.* My unhealthy and misplaced emotional needs were getting met when I felt she needed me.

Here is when the truth really hit home: I am responsible *to*, but not responsible *for*. I am called to be there when she needs a friend, but I am not responsible *for* the decisions she makes. I cannot control her choices, nor can I control the choices of anyone else in my life. I can only control my own choices.

> ## Responsibility
> A person is responsible *to* an individual, but not responsible *for* an individual.

She also cannot make me feel valued just because she needs me (well, she can do whatever she chooses, but I don't have to "play ball" with her if she does). I needed to be reminded that I *am valuable with or without helping others.*

I enabled this friend not by agreeing with her bad decisions, but by allowing her unhealthy, continued dependence on me. I came to her rescue, listened and offered advice she didn't want or take—her mind was already made up. Yet I wanted to be "the strong one" in the friendship because being strong made me feel worthwhile.

Fear of Rejection

These past hurts and pains had also prevented my ability to be vulnerable—for fear of rejection. Old tapes in my head said not to be vulnerable. Don't open up and show 'the real you,' they won't accept you." It didn't feel good.

The wounding I had experienced (and no doubt had caused for others) prevented me from experiencing truly intimate and enjoyable friendships. I was also holding myself back from embracing all that friendship was meant to be.

As I healed I recalled friendships I had sabotaged out of fear of rejection. I remembered discarding a precious friend because I sensed she was pulling back, (when she wasn't at all.) I never asked if something was wrong. I just wrote her off. My fear of her rejection prevented me from when she needed me!

I didn't ask, because I feared being rejected—which probably wasn't true at all. My fear kept me from loving her—and made me self-focused—not a healthy pattern of communication. Although I felt initially disheartened by my destructive patterns, I soon became excited! I was changing my life! I no longer wanted fears to dictate my choices. My friends from here in would be healthy and enlightened. We would be mysteriously drawn to each other (like ships in the night) because we both had worked hard on choosing healthier friendships. We would be *friendship bonded* on the same level, and we would be less likely to hurt one another in conventional, unhealthy ways. Moving from friend-ships to friend-life boats!

Learning to Forgive

As I understood friendship more clearly I began using discernment in choosing friends and could now approach other women with wisdom and love. I forgave those who had hurt me—in part because I now saw the tremendous benefits that had come from those experiences. Without that pain, I would not have learned what it meant to be a purpose-based friend!

I reflected again on previous mistakes and felt horrible I had not thanked a best friend for throwing me a surprise birthday party. (I was too embarrassed at the time to appreciate it.) I regretted dating the ex-boyfriend of another close friend (whoops!). And I felt bad for choosing the fun party over sitting in the hospital with my friend that was in need.

But I knew not to dwell. To heal and grow, I had to let it all go! So I chose to also *forgive myself*. I chose to free myself from guilt because I couldn't change the past; I could only approach the present differently.

Funnily, as I realized my imperfections, I also realized my buddies were imperfect too! It was so liberating!

And then the most unexpected thing happened:

I was suddenly drawn to friendships I would never have expected or sought out myself. It was as if an Invisible Hand came and began to link me with those who wanted the same things from friendship.

From that moment, instead of basing my friendships on beauty, power, prestige, and excitement, I sought friends who were safe. I could entrust my heart to them because *they were trustworthy.*

Please understand: I know nobody is perfect and I still get hurt. It's just that now I try not to own other peoples' issues and no longer carry offenses around like old baggage. I have forgiven, and I am learning how to love my friends with proper boundaries.

New Friendships

As I sought new friendships with a purpose-based foundation, I could distinguish between a *new* friendship based on a foundation of love, truth, and grace versus *old* friendships based mostly on shared commonalities or the desire to have my own needs met. I was compromising my friendship standards because we had children the same age or, because I wanted to be within certain social circles. I began feeling the freedom of an authentic friendship during a difficult season instead of trying to figure it all out for myself.

As you will see in Chapter 6, this led to authenticity in my friendships and realistic expectations of my friends. This produced an entire new friendship world! And the best part is that *I know* that it was worth every second of the pain and heartache to get there.

Your Journey

Do you offer a safe friendship to others? Circle one.

Yes   No

To help you answer the above, consider the following questions:

Knowing that you dislike back-stabbing gossip, does this prevent you talking behind others' backs?

_____

_____

_____

_____

Have you excluded a friend recently out of spite? Explain.

_____

_____

_____

_____

Have you experienced a safe, loving friendship? Explain.

_____

_____

_____

Have you chosen a friend that was not safe for you? Explain.

_____

_____

_____

_____

Did you see any warning signs that your friend might be unsafe for you? Explain.

_____

_____

_____

_____

Did you learn and grow from this friendship? Explain.

_____

_____

_____

_____

Have you experienced any of the issues listed above (a need for discernment, a fear of rejection, codependency, or unforgiveness), or have you experienced other issues? If so, what are they?

_____

_____

_____

_____

Cite three ways in which you can change unhealthy friendship patterns from the past.

_____

_____

_____

_____

Additional Thoughts:

_____

_____

_____

_____

_____

_____

_____

_____

_____

_____

CHAPTER 6

EXPECTATION ADJUSTMENT

My Journey

As my journey progressed, I found myself offering my friends so much more. I knew my limitations and recognized I cared for and appreciated my friends more deeply. I loved feeling I could trust a friend with my heart, and I felt privileged when a friend confided in me and trusted me with theirs.

Authentic Communication

In choosing safer friends, I experienced real and authentic communication—for the first time in my life! We started doing the most remarkable thing: working together through normal interpersonal relationship issues. These same issues had been present in all of my friendships!

Strangely, we became closer—this was completely new to

me. I once believed if you had a disagreement or conflict with someone, that meant the friendship was done and it was time to move on to the next! Well, not so much anymore—I started seeing with safe people, working it out or hanging in there through the mundane was part of the growing process. And in safe friendships, you don't have to grow all alone!

One afternoon, I decided to share my newfound knowledge with a close mom friend, Stacia. As I shared my strengths I mentioned I was the type of friend who *transitioned*— meaning that I sometimes moved on to a new friend once the "old" friend had served her purpose or I had felt that my purposed had been served in her life. I was proud of this revelation but my friend surprised me with her response. "You are not getting rid of me. I'm not going anywhere— ever. I am not one of your 'transition' friends, she said in a clear but firm voice. "

I thought to myself, "How can she truly mean she's not going anywhere? Not even married couples say they will be there forever and half of all couples end up divorced! After we hung up the phone, I considered the type of friendship commitment she spoke of. I also considered my pattern of guarding myself from rejection. I was queen of protecting my heart, and no friend had ever promised not to leave!

Do you remember that we get to choose our friends? Stacia acted as if I were family. Her friendship with me was not a choice and was unconditional. (For example, *"If you do this, then we'll stay friends, but if you mess up, I'm out."*). I still feel teary when I think of this. *Stacia had chosen me. She loved me for me and it did not matter what I did or didn't do!*

This friend has remained one of the most trust-worthy, loyal, and committed friends I could ever ask for. I still cannot believe that a friend could love me this much. Stacia made me see we are actually created to live together, in community. It is possible to have a long-term, purposed-based friendship.

How She Got There—and How We All Can

My friend Stacia had slowly worked towards building these loving, healthy friendships by learning about her own strengths and identity.

She was secure enough in herself to love freely.

Stacia never feared rejection. Therefore she could boldly proclaim her love for her friends because she saw something special in our friendship and was not afraid to commit to it.

Not every friend will be this lasting — many friendships are seasonal and friendships tend to evolve. Just as I am continually changing and evolving personally, so are my friendships. And often we grow out of friendships because we reposition and refocus ourselves. These changes are good and necessary to maintain a healthy balance in friendship.

Stacia embraced the woman God made her to be and out of that understanding she loved her friends well. That's part of the journey I have been on also—to know and love myself just as I am. Once we achieve this we know how beautiful, special, and loved we are ourselves and this frees us up to love others in a healthy, nurturing way.

Realistic Expectations

But not everyone reaches this healthy and liberating place. For instance, my other friend Sady frets over others' responses (or lack thereof). As I observed the friendships around me, I noticed if someone hurts Sady's feelings,

Megan for example, she will withdraw for a few days (in a passive aggressive manner) just to let Megan know that she is on her short list. This might mean ignoring texts and calls. Even worse, Sady will not tell Megan she upset her or try resolving the problem. However, she will let the group know that Megan is "out of the circle" for the week. I love being with her but I worried she might place me on her "undependable" list, which was easily done if I don't understand her every need as a friend. Her friendship expectations are unrealistic.

My take is that Sady is highly sensitive and is fearful of rejection. If someone fails to promptly return her phone call, she convinces herself the friend doesn't really care about her. Or, if a friend excludes her from a birthday luncheon, in return, she refuses to invite them to her next party. Sandy is unforgiving, wounded and carries grudges. We all feel we walk on a very tight rope.

Observing Sandy however, highlighted my own unrealistic expectations for my friends. I realized (to my horror) I was not that much different from Sady. (Maybe that is why we get along so well!) We both hold one another to such high standards that we do not want to upset each other. It works well—for a time—we both walk on eggshells and were careful not to offend. As I try anticipating her expectations, she is anticipating mine.

This vicious cycle had to come to an end. This wasn't fun. But I decided to take my own inventory, or look honestly at my own weaknesses (unmet needs). I noticed I would remove a friend off my next party list if she omitted me from hers. Instead, I should have invited her to my party, if I wanted her presence. I also saw my expectations of Sady weren't realistic. For instance, how can a busy mother of four check in on me daily? (She can't.) And for me to think I could ditch some friends while remain tight for a lifetime with others was unrealistic too. Friendship takes two, not one.

Realizing I needed to adjust my expectations felt liberating. I wasted less time and had more energy. I understood not all friends would be in it for the long haul, and I could adjust my expectations of them. With appropriate expectations, I was finally free to love my friends for whatever length of time God had them into my life.

I saw I could have a purpose-based friend to whom I did not speak for an entire year. On the other hand, I realized that I might have a superficial friend with whom I talk every day. That's the friendship tide, friends going out, some for no identifiable reason, and others coming in, just when you need them the most.

I also adjusted my expectations of myself as a friend. When I accepted I was human and not superhuman, I set more realistic friendship goals for myself and forgave myself for mistakes. *This* was freedom in friendship!

Your Journey

You have your own expectations, desires and needs of your friendships. Adapting your expectations to best meet their behavior can become one of the most powerful tools in your friendship toolbox. This can provide you with the ability to enjoy a mutual, healthy, and beneficial friendship. It can also free you up to enjoy the company of a self-centered and unreliable friend. You will feel less disappointed and more grateful, *if* you adapt your expectations.

Can you recall placing unrealistic expectations on a friend? Explain.

_____

_____

_____

_____

Has a friend placed unrealistic expectations on you? How did this make you feel? Explain.

_____

_____

_____

Do you expect more than a friend is able to provide?
Explain.

_____

_____

_____

Do you have a friendship that expects more than you are
willing to provide? Explain.

_____

_____

_____

_____

Additional Thoughts:

_____

_____

_____

_____

_____

_____

CHAPTER 7

BASIC NEEDS

My Journey

Although each of us is different, typically we have one shared, basic need: *We all want to be loved and feel valued.*

One childhood memory illustrates. While my family and I shared family dinner with the Smith's, our close family friends, I casually mentioned to the younger daughter, Jody, a planned sleepover that Friday night. We planned to go roller-skating and to a movie! I was so excited!

As I babbled on about my outfit I planned to wear and the friends I'd invited, I noticed Jody acted quiet, sad and dejected. Yet as the meal concluded and the family went home, I thought nothing of it.

The next morning, my mom came into my room. She had just gotten off the phone with Jody's mom and learned Jody was heartbroken she hadn't been invited to Friday's sleepover. "How could you reject her like this?" my mother wanted to know. (Remember my lack of discernment?)

I felt terrible and so confused. I had shared the information about the sleepover because I was excited and Jody was my friend. It never occurred to me she would feel upset she wasn't invited. Jody did not feel loved or significant because I had not taken her feelings into consideration. She had a need, and I did not meet her need that night.

Our Basic Needs and Our Friendships

Author, counselor, and CEO of The Hope Center, June Hunt, believes all humans have the same basic human need for *love, significance, and security*.[3] When these needs are not met, people react differently. Some people feel depressed and bed bound. Some people feel angry while others feign happiness to disguise their hurt. So, friendship is a type of relationship that can help us meet our basic needs.

Safe, healthy friendships can help meet some of our basic needs for love, significance, and security.

As I evaluated my healthy friendships, I realized many of my basic needs were indeed being met — June Hunt was on to something!

When I dug deeper into my current friendships I realized one friend made me feel significant because she identified and encouraged me in my strengths. My friend Stacia, who refused to be one of my "transition" friends met my need for security and made me feel loved unconditionally. I felt secure in her commitment to our friendship. And many of my friends showered love on me through thoughtful gestures – these were sweet reminders of how they loved me.

My needs were also being met by sharing myself with a trustworthy friend. When I confided in Stacia and encouraged her, my needs were fulfilled. It went both ways—she loved and encouraged me and I reciprocated!

Two of the greatest gifts in life are found in giving and receiving love and feeling secure within a friendship.

The Flip Side

Yet not all friends met my three basic needs. In fact, many

inadvertently hurt my sense of security. Sometimes, the trusted friend disappointed by acting in an unloving way. When I experienced these disappointments, I now knew to remind myself it's not personal: *hurt people hurt people.* A person's hurtful response or behavior was not about me.

Typically these women had not experienced their own personal healing and were clueless therefore about how to handle my heart with care. Because of their own unresolved hurts, they could not care well for their own hearts, let alone mine.

Tammy

I knew that Tammy had been hurt in the past. This was clear from our first meeting. We met in yoga class and began chatting right away about various poses and our matching leggings. Our connection was instantaneous. We both felt instant familiarity as though we'd known one another since elementary school. We hung out constantly. That was until Tammy began probing about my boyfriend. I soon figured out that Tammy wasn't actually interested in my friendship; she was much more interested in knowing my boyfriend.

Thankfully, I realized Tammy was looking for validation and attention from men rather than seeking out a purpose-based friend. Although I was disappointed Tammy was not the friend I had hoped, I was proud for seeing the truth before I got hurt. I recognized Tammy would not meet my basic needs.

Kendra

And then, Kendra came along. We also happened to enjoy each other's company. Together, with other mutual friends, we went on weekend mountain getaways, had regular dinner parties, and stayed in shape.

Our group had been hanging out for two or more years, when I learned Kendra had been talking about me behind my back and worse —speaking untruths about me and spreading them around.

I felt extremely upset by the betrayal and did not know how to make it right. Fortunately for me, others soon experienced the same backstabbing behavior from Kendra, and everyone understood she had been lying. Not surprisingly, it was all because of my new boyfriend! Kendra had been "chasing" him since junior high and did not want him to date anyone other than her. Little did she know that he was never interested in her. Clearly, Kendra did not know how to care for herself well, or care for my heart.

What was my take away from this experience? I needed to learn to identify safe and healthy people to ensure my own basic needs are taken into consideration.

The Silver Lining

If you haven't experienced friends as scheming as Tammy or Kendra, that's great. But most of us have had friends who are more interested in what they want than in loving us. Each of us has walked through disappointing friendships. And even with our dear, good friends, we sometimes still get hurt.

So why do we keep trying? Why do we continually enter into relationships when we have been repeatedly hurt? I believe we must put ourselves out there if we are to find purpose-based friends.

Vulnerability is a necessary risk of friendship.

As long as we enter a relationship with another human being—a human being that we cannot control—we open ourselves up to being vulnerable. Vulnerability can bring pain and growth. We must remain open in order to find the good friendships so that we can grow.

My journey into friendship bonding has helped increase my awareness of the types of friends I choose and in doing so I have proper expectations as to what sort of friendships they can offer.

Yes, being vulnerable is risky. Learning about what you can and cannot expect from certain friendships takes time. But the hard work and risk pays off because nothing is more beautiful than bonding with a safe friend that offers love, makes you feel valued, and provides security.

Your Journey

You put yourself out there because the benefit of experiencing purpose-based friendship outweighs the risk of getting hurt.

This vulnerability is a necessary risk of friendship.

Can you think of a time that you have put yourself out there only to find you were rejected in a friendship? Explain.

_____

_____

_____

Do you have a safe, healthy friend that has met your basic needs in friendship? What is this relationship like for you? Explain.

_____

_____

_____

_____

_____

_____

Write down a specific example of when a friend has met one or all of your basic needs.

Your Need for Love:

_____

Your Need for Significance:

_____

Your Need for Security:

_____

Describe a specific situation in which you have met a friend's needs.

Her need for Love:

_____

Her need for Significance:

_____

Her need for Security:

_____

CHAPTER 8

PAY ATTENTION

My Journey

Let me remind you:

If you want to know what you will look like in five years, look at who you are hanging out with today.

If emulating your current friends five years from now scares you, then it's time to reevaluate these friendships. Just as you have learned about different types of friends from this book, so should you be clearer on what type of friend you are to others. Intentionally choosing your friends requires paying attention. If you choose gossipy friends then, chances are the same friends will gossip about you. If you are drawn to social climbers, then you should expect these friends to always have an agenda as they socialize. If you choose a friend that is a caring listener, you can bet that she will want to listen when you need her. If you opt for a funny friend, she will probably make you laugh. As you pay attention to the friendship garden you are cultivating, know that if you plant a rose bush, you cannot expect a tulip to bloom (unless you live with Alice in Wonderland).

As you pay attention and choose friends more purposefully, I hope you notice yourself growing in your friendship choices. In the past, you might have chosen the "exciting" friend; now, you have the chance to choose your friends by wisely discerning who is safe and who is not.

As you change, you will find less interest in friends who might manipulate you for personal gain. Someone like the "bossy Queen Bee" who once impressed you, no longer holds any appeal. Traits that did not impress you before—for instance someone being a good listener, are now attractive.

Debra

Many years ago I met a woman named Debra. For a while, we occasionally ran into one another, but I was never really drawn to her — mainly because I was drawn to the extroverts. She, on the other hand, was normal, introverted, quiet, and reserved. Debra only spoke when someone asked her a question. I preferred the outgoing, make-me-laugh, get-the-job-done types.

Yet little by little we interacted more frequently, and communicated more often. Gradually I got to know her heart. I liked what I saw. Debra was loyal, honest, and trustworthy. She honored her friends, never spoke behind anyone's back, even when I was desperate for details on a topic, she never allowed one friend to pry about another. She would not offer up anything! Debra showed me there are actually people you can trust not to talk behind your back!

As the years drew on *this* drew me to her; not that she was an outgoing, fancy pants (though I did take her shopping after a few months)! This also revealed to me that my intentional choosing of friends was transforming the relationships I was in. My relationship with Debra was an eye-opener. With my newly opened eyes (and my cute new Chanel sunglasses), I was actually changing! It really worked!

Just like your mom and dad told you:
"Pay attention, honey, and choose wisely!

Your Journey

Intentionally choosing whom you allow into your friendship circle is bigger decision than you probably realize. In order to experience purpose-based friendship, you must consciously choose with whom you share your life.

You might still be "friends" with your elementary school buddy, but you might also have grown apart and not feel trust. You might choose a coworker at work whom you feel could become a lifelong friend because she meets your friendship needs. Or, you might be growing alongside a friend that you have known since college, and together you might be learning how to love each other better.

Now is a good time to think about whom you have chosen and are choosing to be your trusted friends!

Have you ever considered that you can be intentional in picking which friends are in and which friends are out? (If you have an unhealthy relationship, you don't have to stay there.) Explain.

_____

_____

_____

Can you examine your motives and discern why you have chosen to invest and spend time with most of your friends? Explain.

_____

_____

_____

_____

Do you sometimes wonder why you are friends with certain people? Explain.

_____

_____

_____

_____

Do you know why you have chosen to be friends with certain people? Share an example.

_____

_____

_____

_____

How can you pay better attention to the types of friends you select? Explain.

_____

_____

_____

Additional Thoughts:

_____

_____

_____

_____

_____

_____

_____

_____

_____

_____

_____

_____

_____

CHAPTER 9

INDIVIDUAL FRIENDSHIP CHOICES

My Journey

As I was beginning to choose intentionally for myself for the first time, I started noticing why other people were choosing certain friends. Initially I felt confused.

I noticed one friend choosing a friend because she had the same-aged children, but otherwise they shared no commonality. I observed another friend choose someone from their childhood. But as adults they did not engage socially at all. Another close friend loves all types of people. She can befriend anyone and does not care about any commonalities—she just loves to love. She loves interacting with an interesting and broad cross-section of people.

So I began to wonder, "Did each person have her own

reason for choosing her friends?" Maybe my new friendship standard was not going to be the same as everyone else's.

Friendship Measuring Stick

I was realizing friendship is more complex and difficult to define than a list of qualities and characteristics, in part because each person defines friendship differently. Most women have different types of friends. One woman believes that being a friend means that someone is available for her when she is in crisis. Another woman considers a friend to be someone she has known for years. For another, a friend is someone who knows her secrets and doesn't judge her.

So, just like every person has unique strengths and talents, so every person has a different perspective as to who they call *friend*.

Bridgette

Bridgette was a recent college graduate in her mid-twenties. She just started a new job as a recruiter at a reputable law firm in Texas. I also recruited at the same firm. We worked closely together, helping bring in new law school graduates.

Although I would not seek any life or boyfriend advice from Bridgette, we enjoyed socializing after work. I considered Bridgette a friend.

Jenna

Jenna and I, on the other hand, have been good friends for fifteen years; in fact, we grew up down the street from each other. We were both cheerleaders and track stars. As young adults, we connected through our love for cooking and by taking joint culinary classes. We traded information about our daily lives and shared hobbies. Even though I did not share truly intimate details with Jenna, I certainly considered her a good friend and could count on her for almost anything.

Christie

And then there's Christie. We met on a playground while we were pushing our children on the swing set. As we started talking, we realized much in common! In no time I felt comfortable opening up to Christie; I intuitively knew Christie was wise beyond her years. After that first conversation, we started meeting regularly at the park.

It wasn't long before we introduced our husbands over dinner. Soon, all four of us were friends. We continued spending time together regularly, and although we have only known each other for a year, we trust each other and help each other. Our friendship bond has fulfilled a need both of us had as young women.

Each of my friends depicted above I met in different environments and each fulfilled different friendship needs, but none is a greater friend than the other.

So it seems we all have different types of friends, and our different friends fill different needs in our lives . . .

This revelation felt exciting—I could open myself up to various friends from varying walks of life. Whereas before I might discriminate against those who weren't "fun enough," now I could see that an "un-fun" friend might be just who I need on a cloudy day. Freedom in my friendships was soon to follow.

Friendship Compartments

As I opened myself up to different types of friendships, I

also opened myself up to greater learning.

One friend called to ask if she could come over. I gladly rearranged my day to sit and chat about all her problems and brainstorm about solutions. I enjoyed her visual excitement as she had her own epiphanies on what to do. She would tell me how wise she thought I was. She would say that I was better than her paid counselors.

All was well until one day she said, "You know that I am just coming to you for advice, don't you?" I processed this to mean; she was only coming to me to listen to her problems. Once those problems were over, she would no longer come. Previously this would have alarmed me and made me question the longevity of our friendship. I would have had to process for weeks. However, my response was so different — I had already categorized this friend as someone whom I enjoyed helping, and with no strings attached. Sharing my wisdom is a gift I enjoy giving, so I was free to help her without expecting to be close friends. This was an "assigned friend." My role was to help her through this season with nothing in return. So any rejection therefore would not be personal.

I have learned not to expect a friend who is not a nurturer to care for me when I am sick. I can ask the friend that loves to "save the day" to help me during a crisis but I should probably not expect her to spearhead my birthday party.

Realizing every friendship serves a different purpose felt liberating. Understanding which category each of my friends fell into redirected my expectations instead of disappointing me. I gave grace to the friend that was constantly late and forgave the friend that only called because she needed something.

Finally, a few, very close, very trustworthy friends arose and fell nicely into my "highly trusted" compartment. These are the friends I can call in the middle of night. We pray together and share with one another any marital or other private difficulties. These friends are my inner circle — the ones to whom I go for the most intimate of advice. And since I chose this inner circle so carefully, these have remained the most faithful friends I could ever want. Of course, disappointments and misunderstandings arise now and then — nobody is perfect —but now, I can see we are all committed to being as honest and open and true as we can possibly be.

I'm sharing with you some friendship compartments I use in my own life to help you identify different roles for your own friends. You will probably find your friends fall into multiple compartments — no friend is confined to one. In fact, many will transition between several compartments. .

The Acquaintance

- You know each other by name.

- You say hello.

- You like each other, but you would not arrange a lunch together.

The Comfy Friend

- You are comfortable enough to hug and talk when you see each other.

- Your conversation remains superficial. You talk mainly about common interests and daily life.

The Assigned Friend

- This friendship is one that you are called to or "assigned to" for a certain reason or purpose.

- This friendship usually lasts a season.

- You love sacrificially while the assigned friend learns and grows from what you have to offer.

The Close Friend

- You desire to make an extra effort.

- You share with one another your deeper cares and concerns, joys and victories.

- Trust is present.

The Best Friend

- You consider this friend to be one of your best.

- You have a deep level of trust.

- You share memories.

- You make an effort to be together.

- You really like her as a person.

The Purpose-Based Friend

- This friendship is like a breath of fresh air.

- This friendship is not perfect, but it is intentional. You both are aware of how the other person is doing, feeling, thinking, and living.

- Both friends must be trustworthy, speak truthfully, and both must honor and respect the other person, even in her weaknesses.

- This friendship reciprocates, sacrifices, loves, gives and takes, and nourishes.

- Both friends encourage and uplift each other when they see the other person's strengths shining.

- You genuinely want the best for one another.

Once I identified whom I needed to place where, I was able to love *all of them* more freely. I no longer expected a close friend to be a trusted friend when her biggest weakness was gossip, but I could still love and be her friend. I simply must remain guarded and not bear my soul to her as I would a trusted friend.

The level of friendship that we offer another reflects our internal character. You may be an acquaintance to one friend and a close friend to another. The compartments into which you place your friendships don't need to influence the type of friend you are to others. The truth is, you cannot be a purpose-based friend to one person and untrustworthy to another. If your character is honest and faithful, then you will be honest and faithful to all your friends! Be authentic, be who you are.

For me, one of the greatest gifts in friendship is having the power to choose whom we let in. We can take our own inventory and examine our heart to see what we want out of our friendships. Once we understand our needs, we obtain the privilege of choosing accordingly. What a gift to be able to choose whom we call friend!

The Friendship Bond, Dates with Friends

Companion Book

In the accompanying book, *The Friendship Bond, Dates with Friends*, you can read about a variety of different friends types you may have encountered in your journey. You may have met The Broadway Friend, The Sweet Heart, or The Popular Friend along the way. The ideal friend is The Purpose-Based Friend. She is a combination of the best traits from all friend types, as well as, a unique blessing all her own.

Your Journey

Throughout your life you've been blessed to choose your friends. Some arrived unexpectedly, while others seemed like part of a master plan.

What traits do your close, best, or trusted friends possess?

☐	Listens to you	☐	Compassionate
☐	Puts you first	☐	Encouraging
☐	Trustworthy	☐	Supportive
☐	Empathetic	☐	Affirming
☐	Merciful	☐	Secure
☐	Honest	☐	Loving
☐	Patient	☐	Loyal
☐	Kind	☐	Good
☐	Gentle with your heart	☐	Thoughtful

Does the list of friendship compartments help you to determine where to place certain friends? Explain.

_____

_____

_____

Does having a "compartment mentality" when it comes to friends help you have more realistic expectations? Explain.

_____

_____

_____

What compartments would you create for your own friendships?

_____

_____

_____

Additional Thoughts:

_____

_____

_____

_____

CHAPTER 10

GIVING AND RECEIVING

My Journey

I have learned how to view my friendships by categorizing them appropriately. This helps me discern to whom I will give and from whom I will receive. The first is easier for me, giving. I love to give gifts, throw parties, and listen. I love stewarding my time, talent, and treasure appropriately.

I love seeing my friends smiling face when I bring her the hard-to-find eye cream she sought. I love knowing that Ugandan orphans are eating and drinking better partly because of my charity work. I love hugging people. I love giving my time to purposeful friendships. And yes, I love giving my two cents worth. Does that also count?

I love the ripple effect that giving has in the world. Whenever we give with the right motives (and sometimes even the wrong ones), we set in motion a ripple effect.

Every wave created arrives at the shore, no matter how distant.

Please don't think I am an extremely noble person — actually, I struggle giving when I feel obligated or manipulated. Nor do I enjoy giving when my gift requires actually sacrificing something for myself. (I'm still maturing, remember?).

As for those giving around me...

Friends and family have shown me how life would be if we expected nothing in return. I cannot think of one time that my brother has not swooped in, helped out, served and loved his friends and family. I feel this way about my sister-in- laws as well. They all come in to help, swiftly and unconditionally, expecting nothing back. Each of them amazes me. These people are an inspiration to many.

Strings Attached

Although I see many within my community giving selflessly, some around me are also un-giving and self absorbed, (and sometimes this includes myself.) For the first ten years of marriage, my husband and I both kept tally marks of all we did for our young child. We counted the numbers of diapers changed, bedtime books read, and afternoon trips to the park. In retrospect we both realized "keeping score" wasted our time and energy. After all, we were both the parents. Thankfully, we broke this pattern and altered our thoughts and hearts so that helping each other came from wanting to bless that person, not so that we could gain a "return on our investment." I witnessed this pattern of people giving with strings attached throughout my life. If one person did a favor, she expected one in return. I witnessed this in school, friendship, business, and charity work.

Observing that everyone's giving had some kind of agenda saddened me — I didn't want to be a "strings attached" type of friend. I wanted to give freely and unconditionally without expecting anything back and without causing any friend to question my motives. I decided simply not to ask for help. If I needed help, I would do it myself. As time progressed, I came to understand that this approach made it very difficult for me to receive. I had become independent and taken pride in the fact that I did not "need" anyone. Really, I needed help. I not only needed others in my life to help me when I could not help myself but I was missing out on a very important part of life: The ability to receive. I also needed to receive joyfully instead of feeling inadequate (or a bother) for not doing the job myself.

No Strings Attached

I knew relationships are greatly enhanced if we give and receive graciously, in tandem with one another in order for the blessings to flow. Yet I still struggled with receiving generosity and kindness from others. I was much more comfortable with giving. Eventually my friends forced my hand. One sunny afternoon in Texas, my doorbell rang. When I answered however no one was there – only an empty porch — but at my feet was a beautifully wrapped gift. I knew today was not my birthday and when I brought the gift inside all I could do was look at it. I finally opened the box to find a fabulous soup maker. This was not just any soup maker. It was a Mercedes of soup makers! And it was not even my birthday! But, instead of being excited, I felt guilty. I could not accept this fancy gift. My friend had given it to me as a "thank you" for loving and caring tenderly for her heart. No other reason. I was shocked by how much I struggled with this spontaneous act of generosity and yet I knew if I were to truly engage in purposeful friendships I needed to graciously receive kindness as well as give it.

I must learn to look at things from the giver's perspective and understand that it gives good people joy to give. So let them give!

I was equally tested at a dinner party one fall when another friend from my college days, Angie, won the most beautiful diamond cross bracelet in a raffle the night before. I expounded on how beautiful it was and my amazement it was donated to a raffle. Angie urged me to try it on, which I dutifully did, hoping my husband would perhaps notice how gorgeous it looked on me and buy me one of my own.

My friend surprised me by saying she wanted me to keep it! I protested hotly. But she was undeterred. She absolutely wanted me to have it, and surprisingly without asking anything in return.

I was awestruck and speechless not only by my friend's kindness but also by her lack of materialism. Who does that? Not me! Remember, I love my creature comforts—I am not that nice.

Angie challenged my understanding of what it meant to give; she moved it up a level (or ten!). But could I accept the gift? I would've felt too guilty. I did, however, happily wear it the next day—all day long—to the hairdresser, to pick up my son at school, to meet my husband for lunch, to dinner that night with friends. Then I returned it. The best part, years later, I received a beautiful diamond cross bracelet. And this one was from my husband!

The Reality of Giving and Receiving

I would like to say I overcame my inability to receive kindness but alas, I have not. Even when a friend writes me a thoughtful note, I feel guilty of the time it took her to write. What is wrong with me?!

Where I have improved however is I now see the importance of giving and taking in healthy friendships. This is why I continue working on becoming a better receiver. I am a living example of a "work in progress."

Your Journey

Giving and receiving is a healthy part of any friendship. The ability to embrace both giving and receiving within friendship is a beautiful thing!

Do you believe that it is better to give or to receive? Explain.

_____

_____

_____

Do you believe that it is better to be blessed or to have the power to bless? Explain.

_____

_____

_____

Do you have a friend that is a better giver than receiver? Explain.

_____

_____

_____

Do you have a friend that is a better receiver than a giver? Explain.

_____

_____

_____

In your friendships, are you a better giver or receiver? Explain.

_____

_____

_____

When was the last time you gave unconditionally to a friend? Explain.

_____

_____

_____

Additional Thoughts:

_____

_____

_____

_____

_____

_____

_____

CHAPTER 11

RECIPROCATING

My Journey

Please note, this process of learning more about myself and my friendships has taken years and years! It's been over two decades since I first met my first angel, Anna on the front steps of my home as a young girl. I am constantly reminded we all just want to be loved and we are all imperfect. I see how much I have learned, and how far I have to go. I have grown in friendship, yet I long to be an even better friend. I want to love and care tenderly for those hearts that God has entrusted to me.

I realize there are seasons in which I walk closely with certain friends, and then seasons in which we are apart. I now understand this is meant to be that way. Another friend will teach me something new, and hopefully I teach them too. We mustn't cling to anyone or anything, nor should we try to control them or their behavior. All I can control is my response.

Reciprocating

We can respond however we want to friendship. We don't need to feel out of control. As Newton would say, "For every action there is a reaction."

Reciprocate
To give and take *mutually*.

This leads me to my next point: How am I reacting? If a friend takes the time to listen to my woes, is that all that I am doing? What is my part in this friendship? Am I reciprocating?

I remember an old wise man named Lou, the father of a close high school friend, once told me to *always give back from where I take.* I have not always done this in friendships. Sometimes I would lean on my wisest friends for wisdom and then ditch or ignore them when my problem was solved. I thought only about my own needs – not theirs. When I was less enlightened, I believed these friends needed nothing from me. But that was a lie. The truth was every friend needed something I uniquely had to offer. I might have not known what it was, and she might never have asked, but needs were present on both sides. I had not fulfilled my role in friendship.

I needed to reciprocate.

Even if I could not come close to matching her divine wisdom, I could send an encouraging letter; drop a casserole off on her doorstep. I could call her just to check in (not for advice).

I learned there is a life cycle, if I choose to participate. It is like we have been ordained since the beginning of time to live and breathe with this cycle:

THE CYCLE OF HELPING YOURSELF,

THEN OTHERS,

AND THEN THE WORLD.

Practicing reciprocity will not only benefit your friendships, but it will also spill over into other areas of your life. As you become more sensitive to this give-and-take mentality, you will want to serve more, help more, and follow through more with those promptings that are placed on your heart.

You will possess a heightened awareness as to when you are taking more than your fair share. What was comfortable in the past in this area will no longer be appropriate for you. You will want to give back from where you take.

Operating from your strengths and your temperament will enable you to reciprocate more easily. This will be done with a heart of joy and a sense of purpose. You will cease to be inwardly focused. Your gaze will face outward towards others. The cycle of experiencing friendship to its fullest includes a heavy dose of reciprocity!

Your Journey

Examine your friendships; are they reciprocal? Explain.

_____

_____

_____

Do you try giving back from where you have taken? Explain.

_____

_____

_____

Do you work together with your friends to help the world around you? Explain.

_____

_____

_____

Cite your strengths. How can you utilize these strengths to bless a giving and kind friend in your life? Explain.

_____

_____

_____

_____

_____

Which newly discovered strengths can you now put to good use? Explain.

_____

_____

_____

_____

Additional Thoughts:

_____

_____

_____

_____

_____

_____

_____

_____

_____

_____

_____

CHAPTER 12

BALANCE AND BOUNDARIES

My Journey

At this point in my purpose-based friendship journey, I was feeling good. I was making positive changes in my relationships. I was giving with pure motives and more cognizant of my strengths and those in my friends. Slowly but surely, I was learning to reciprocate.

The only drawback was I was giving so much, I felt exhausted. I was making myself too available and helping others too much. I convinced myself I wouldn't be a great friend, unless I constantly gave and yet this pattern was unhealthy.

My Glowing Friend

On one gloomy, rainy February day in Texas, I was on the way to meet my "glowing" friend. I wasn't sure how upbeat I would be. I felt completely burned out from helping everyone — my friends, my son, my son's friends – pretty much everyone I knew had been the recipient of some kind deed I had performed. In walked Miss Glowing, with a beautiful, radiant smile and a spring to her step. Her perspective was positive . . . what a breath of fresh air for me on that cold, dark February day!

After that startling day in the coffee shop, where her attitude and mine seemed as different as carrots and whipped cream, I paid attention to her living her life in balance. Even in challenging circumstances she remains positive and upbeat. She doesn't sweat the small stuff. She lives in a place that is the *opposite* of chaos.

She makes a concerted effort to purpose-base her friendships and to love herself. She has time to listen, and you enjoy her company because she has so much to give. I look forward to being with her because she rubs off on me. I leave her presence a better person.

Another quality I've observed in Miss Glowing is her ability to say no, or yes, to any request. She knows how to give and take. She doesn't internalize or worry about circumstances she cannot control.

She has a strong sense of self, is confident in her identity, and owns her strengths. She has her friendship compartments wired tight. She knows which friend is assigned, which one is close, which one is best, and which one should remain an acquaintance. She even knows who might be switching from comfy to best friend before the switch actually happens!

She lets God meet her needs for love, significance, and security so she is always "filled up" and able to "pour out" for others. When she can't see the truth for herself on hormonal or blue days, she knows which friends will offer encouragement.

Boundaries

After admiring her many strengths and ability to manage life with great ease and peace, I noticed that Miss Glowing is skilled at placing firm boundaries around her relationships.

Relationship experts and co-authors of the best selling book titled *Boundaries*, Dr. Henry Cloud and Dr. John Townsend define a boundary as a personal property line that marks those things for which we

> ## Boundary
>
> A personal property line that marks those things for which we are responsible.
>
> Defines who we are and who we are not.

are responsible. These experts believe a person should place different types of boundaries in their life. These boundaries are physical, mental, emotional, and spiritual.

- A **physical** boundary designates *who* can touch us and *under what circumstances.*

- A **mental** boundary gives us the freedom to *think for ourselves* and form our own opinions.

- An **emotional** boundary helps us *manage our emotions* and *separates us* from the manipulative and injury-causing emotions of others.

- A **spiritual** boundary will help us to discern God's desires for our lives from our own desires for our lives.[4]

It is these qualities I observed in "glowing" friend that separated her from the rest of the pack. She knew her limitations! She operated from a place of peace because she had learned how to place healthy boundaries in her life.

No wonder I gleefully anticipated our coffee dates! She modeled for me what it would look like to live and breathe a balanced life. She modeled for me that I did not have to say yes to an invitation when I needed to say no. She showed me I did not have to fear hurting someone's feelings if I knew I would be compromising my own boundary; or if I pulled back from a codependent friend. I deeply desired Miss Glowing's ability to place healthy boundaries between herself and her friends and gradually I began emulating her techniques so I could become healthier in friendships and feel less burned out.

Your Journey

Do you value living a balanced life? Explain.

_____

_____

_____

Do you have areas in your life that are not balanced?
Explain.

_____

_____

_____

Describe one area in which you can enforce a boundary (if
needed).

_____

_____

_____

How do you think this person (or situation) would be
impacted if you set a firm boundary? Explain.

_____

_____

_____

_____

Prepare for Implementing New Boundaries

• If you choose to create and enforce a new boundary, prepare yourself ahead of time. Know that you are now changing the "rules of the game" with the other person by putting up a new boundary. If you understand that this person may not respond favorably, her response will be easier to manage. Stay strong— enforcing new, healthy boundaries always leads to growth and freedom!

• Asking a very trusted friend or family member to help you (if needed) to enforce a boundary might be necessary in some instances.

Additional Thoughts:

_____

_____

_____

_____

_____

_____

CHAPTER 13

THE GRACE AWAKENING

My Journey

As you have learned, there are many aspects to friendship. People are complex, so why would friendship be any different? People are also imperfect, so why would friendship be any different?

I officially decided that we each have our own garden to cultivate and that we only get the privilege of cultivating one garden—*our own.*

What do I mean by this? For starters, I can't judge another person for bringing her life experience, hardships, upbringing, issues, or past choices into how she views and handles friendship. I am not implying just because I don't get to weed another's garden means I have to engage in close and unhealthy friendships. Not at all!

But I can reflect back on the ways I carried my own fears and insecurities into my friendships and acknowledge others probably will do the same. Furthermore, not everyone has the desire, willingness, or ability to dive into this topic as I have. (Perhaps that is why I'm writing this book!)

Therefore, I cannot judge another friend's actions. I might never know why some people till their soil and plant seeds for roses while others prefer hydrangeas. *I might value orchids (loyalty) while another values peonies (time).*

Although we have the same basic needs, we all have unique differences. This makes life a blast! People are also subject to change (growth). Therefore, we should never write anyone off. We must offer grace to our friends at all times.

Freedom to Change	Offering grace allows us to give others the freedom to grow and transform. This is why we don't "write anyone off" - but continue to place boundaries when necessary.

Grace offered is like a peaceful, clear water stream that flows through beautiful snow capped mountains on a warm summer's day. This grace-giving rapid is always needed, welcomed, and hopefully present.

First, Grace Frees Us from Unforgiveness

Unforgiveness is like that stubborn ten pounds we cannot lose. We don't like its heaviness, but we struggle with how to let it go.

Grace	An extension of mercy and forgiveness even when it is not requested.

As we offer *grace* to ourselves for our mistakes and let ourselves off the "perpetual guilty" mindset treadmill, we can forgive ourselves. We know we are not perfect—so why expect perfection and chastise ourselves for our shortcomings?

Forgiveness allows amazing things to take shape. You relinquish anger and resentment towards yourself and others. And before you know it, that stubborn ten pounds disappears. Offering grace to yourself is the first step in extending forgiveness to others.

Second, Grace Gives Us the Ability to Extend Forgiveness

Forgiving is a gift. You will feel liberated and like a brand new person. Although often the choice to forgive others has to be done without their asking for it, your forgiveness will part the heavens and let the light shine down on your soul! Like a refreshing spring rain, you will breathe more freely.

Rest assured even the best of friendships have endured conflict and disappointment. These friendships tackled challenges and responded in love and with humility. These are the types of friendship we all aspire to have.

My desire is to readily offer grace. No matter what type of friend has hurt us, extend grace because we need it ourselves. There is no "perfect" friend.

Your Journey

Grace is a wonderful gift to offer your friendships. It feels liberating to relinquish judgment and forgive a past hurt.

Is there a friend from whom you need to extend grace or forgiveness? Explain.

_____

_____

_____

Is there a friend that you need to ask for forgiveness? Explain.

_____

_____

_____

Are there other areas in your life in which you have been harboring resentment or bitterness? Explain.

_____

_____

_____

_____

_____

CHAPTER 14

SELF-REFLECTION

Your Journey

You have put your heart, time, and energy into this process. Take a deep breath, and think about your experiences. Reflect on your notes and recall the high points.

You have learned about owning your own strengths, recognizing and choosing to value the traits of a safe person, growing into being a safe person yourself, giving and receiving, compartmentalizing, and extending grace and forgiveness. As you embrace these principles and exercise these foundations, you will experience a new way of bonding in friendship.

Looking at the type of friend we truly are to others is the most important piece to the puzzle. We cannot expect others to provide for us what we are not willing to give.

We cannot expect someone to be a purpose-based friend
until we become a purpose-based friend to ourselves.

Let's re-examine what friendship really looks like in your life.

To be a purpose-based friend, you must understand yourself. As you have learned more about your individual strengths and qualities, have you found yourself wanting to be a better friend yourself? Explain.

_____

_____

_____

The more secure you become in yourself,
the easier it is to love other people for who they are.

Has your vision become clearer as you have learned every friend is not meant to be a purpose-based friend? Explain.

_____

_____

_____

Do you agree that you can choose friends for different reasons? Explain.

_____

_____

_____

What type of friend are you to others? Explain.

_____

_____

_____

Do you place realistic or unrealistic expectations on your friends? Explain.

_____

_____

How would you like to improve your existing friendships? Explain.

_____

_____

_____

What have you learned about yourself that you did not know or see prior to reading this book? Explain.

_____

_____

_____

What have you learned about yourself as a friend? Explain.

_____

_____

_____

_____

Which of the Purpose-Based Friend traits do you possess?

☐	Listen to others	☐	Compassionate
☐	Put others first	☐	Encouraging
☐	Trustworthy	☐	Supportive
☐	Empathetic	☐	Affirming
☐	Merciful	☐	Secure
☐	Honest	☐	Loving
☐	Patient	☐	Loyal
☐	Kind	☐	Good
☐	Gentle with their hearts	☐	Thoughtful

What have you learned about your friendships? Explain.

_____

_____

_____

_____

_____

What has been your favorite part of this journey? Explain

_____

_____

_____

_____

How has this process impacted your heart? Explain.

_____

_____

How do you want to change or grow as a result? Explain.

_____

_____

_____

_____

_____

_____

_____

Describe new strengths you have found in yourself during this process.

_____

_____

_____

_____

_____

_____

In what ways did you receive confirmation that you are on the right track? Explain.

_____

_____

_____

_____

_____

Did you have previous self-doubts or fears that you feel you have overcome during this process? Explain.

_____

_____

_____

_____

_____

How have you grown into becoming a better friend? Explain.

_____

_____

_____

_____

_____

_____

Have you been inspired to make positive changes? Explain.

_____

_____

_____

_____

Additional Thoughts:

_____

_____

_____

_____

_____

_____

CHAPTER 15

PURPOSE-BASED THINKING

My Journey

I believe we can only offer to others that which we first possess ourselves. I have found that learning about my own identity, personality, strengths, and weaknesses allows me to see the good in myself. In turn, I also now see the good in others more frequently and have a greater capacity to give my friends the love, care, and encouragement they need.

I continue to learn, let go, and change. I am constantly experiencing friendship growth and lessons in friendship. These "friendship lessons" have actually changed me as a wife and mother and have even made me a better acquaintance. Isn't that the nature of true change? When we choose to learn and grow in one area, it spills over into others.

I am far from perfect as a friend but I have gained a clearer understanding of my weaknesses. I now realize being a friend means being fully present, and I am much more selective with whom I become close to. The old me sought close connections with everyone. This resulted in everyone getting a watered-down, spread-thin, Melanie. Now, in my careful choosing, my close friends get a Melanie who is "all in" with them. Let me list all the ways in which I feel I've grown:

- I am thankful for all I am learning about myself and my friendships.

- I am thankful I am learning to recognize which friends will help grow me into the woman I have been created to become.

- I am thankful that my friends give me the freedom and grace to continually work on growing in purposed-based friendship.

The Roman thinker Cicero once said, *"Friendship makes prosperity brighter, while it lightens adversity by sharing its grief and anxieties."*

I love my new way of thinking about friendship . . . with purpose!

Your Journey

I hope and pray that you will benefit and connect with yourself and your friends in new ways after your journey through *The Friendship Bond*.

If you wish to start a journey of discovery with a group of friends, I recommend reading the *Dates with Friends*, Message from Melanie and the details about the *Dates with Friends* companion book.

the
friendship
band
dates with friends

COMPANION BOOK

MESSAGE FROM MELANIE

A date is a scheduled time to spend with another person or people. I love having a lunch date with my son, a dinner date with my husband, or a coffee date with my close girlfriend. This is a time for connecting. We usually start out updating one another on what is going on in our lives then we dive into deeper level chitchat. We share from our hearts about victories, struggles, experiences, perspectives, and life.

Many years ago, my friend Stacey started a dinner club—only girls allowed. We showed up at her house in our pajamas and enjoyed a home spa night. At another friend's house we played charades while another friend would cook us dinner. We would enjoy a delicious meal and set her table with her finest china and linens. Our time together was purposeful. We did not gossip. We encouraged, loved, and supported one another in marriage, parenting, and business. We were honest and open about our struggles. We celebrated in one another's victories. These are some of my favorite memories with some of my dearest friends. Spending regular time with these women formed a lifelong bond between us. Today, most of us are mothers, some of our husbands have come and gone (some have stayed), many of us have added more laugh lines and we all joke we have not remained the same dress size. Even if we don't reunite frequently, I still feel close to them because of this time of togetherness. Friendship bonds were formed.

Before Stacey's dinner club, I believed time with friends would either be a night of deep chitchat or an evening of silly, spontaneous fun. I would choose which friends I would "go on a date with" depending on my mood. Stacey made me see I could have both! I also realized that my favorite time with friends combines laughter with vulnerability.

Dates with Friends, the companion book to *The Friendship Bond*, is meant to capture this ideal: dates filled with laughter, bonding, and a safe place to be vulnerable. This book is meant to encourage and guide women who want to learn, grow, and experience life and friendship in new ways. Just as Stacey enlightened me towards this path, so I hope *Dates with Friends* does this for you and your friends!

May each of you on this journey build bonds with those friends that you value and hold so dear to your heart! And for those stepping out and taking a risk by including friends you don't know too well, what a remarkable place to be! Your life will not only be enriched, but you will bless these other women in new and meaningful ways. Opening up your group to women you don't know as well is a reflection of your willingness to get out of your comfort zone and share your own life with others!

On this journey, remember:

- There will never be another you to share with others.

- There will never be another day like today.

- There will never be another bond like each of the ones you are about to form!

INTRODUCTION

You are about to embark on an unforgettable journey. You will make memories, laugh, and learn more about yourself and others along the way.

If you are reading *Dates with Friends* with a group of friends, each person will also need a copy of *The Friendship Bond*. *The Friendship Bond* will provide background to each date in this book and will prepare each person for your group discussions!

In *The Friendship Bond* and *Dates with Friends*, you will learn about your individual identity and personality, experience purposeful conversations and careful self-reflection, and get to do all of this with your friends while having FUN!

Together you will explore the meaning and purpose of friendship. You will consider your personal perspective on friendship and what friendship means to you. You will answer questions like:

- Are you maturing in the way you relate to your friends?

- Are you finding friendships no longer work for you while others spring up in unexpected places?

- Do you know how to choose friends that look after your best interest rather than trying to tear you down?

- What type of friend are you to others?

By the end of this process, you will have learned new things about yourself and see yourself and others in a new light that broadens and enriches your own life as well as the lives of your friends. Now get ready, because you are about to embark on a friendship adventure unlike any other!

THE FORMAT

As a group, you will go through *The Friendship Bond* and use the *Dates with Friends* companion book to spur on conversations and instigate insightful discussions. This companion book is divided into three parts. The different dates laid out in Part III each correspond to the chapters in *The Friendship Bond*.

Part I: The Friendex

In Part I and Part II you will decide which friends will be a part of the journey with you! Before you officially form your group, you will read through different Friend Types that you may have encountered in your friendship experiences. These are intended to generate thought, laughs, and help you form your list.

Part II: The Group

You will learn to discern which friends—old and new—you should include in your group! Then, together, you all will continue through Part III.

Part III: The Dates

Each date in this companion book corresponds with the chapters in *The Friendship Bond*. It will be important for each person in your group to have and bring *The Friendship Bond* book and this companion book on each date!

You are encouraged to discuss how to tailor your dates to meet the needs of your group. If your time is limited, you might want to come up with an alternative to the assignment provided. This group is meant to be a blessing, not a burden.

The hope is that, in the end you have had an experience with your friends that will cultivate bonding, promote connection, build memories, and transform the way you view friendship. You will feel better equipped with tools and insights to draw you closer to the women in your group, as well as, in your life. You will be given a framework for bringing purposeful fun and play into your friendships!

About Melanie

Melanie grew up in Dallas, Texas. She gained her bachelor's degree in teaching with a minor in theater arts at the University of Texas at Austin. She furthered her education by taking master's level courses in counseling and temperament analysis. Little did Melanie know that her education and life experiences would one day inspire her to create the *Life Bonds* connection books.

Already living a life of meaning and satisfaction, Melanie wants others to share her journey through purposeful exchanges on subjects of friendship, motherhood, marriage, and family. She sees her wisdom as "gifts" to initiate new ways of thinking about life. Melanie's material is positive, fun, challenging and heartwarming.

FOR MORE *LIFE BONDS* CONNECTIONS:

f   The Friendship Bond

f   My Life Bonds

t   @melrossmills

t   @friendship_bond

◉   melanierossmills

www.melanierossmills.com

www.mylifebonds.com

coming soon . . .

in the works . . .

Notes

Chapter 5: Safe or Unsafe

[1] Henry Cloud and John Townsend, *Safe People* (Grand Rapids, Michigan: Zondervan, 1995), 21.

[2] Ibid, 21-24.

Chapter 7: Basic Needs

[3] June Hunt, Hope for The Heart. www.hopefortheheart.org.

Chapter 12: Balance and Boundaries

[4] Henry Cloud and John Townsend, Boundaries (Grand Rapids, Michigan: Zondervan, 1992).

Made in the USA
Charleston, SC
06 May 2014